Boy in Various Poses

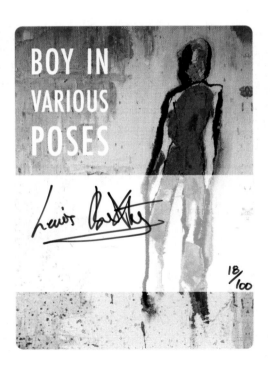

Boy in Various Poses

Lewis Buxton

Nine
Arches
Press

Boy in Various Poses
Lewis Buxton

ISBN: 9781913437138
eISBN: 9781913437145

Cover artwork: 'Them' © Anita Staff
www.ffatsatina.com

First published May 2021 by:

Nine Arches Press
Unit 14, Sir Frank Whittle Business Centre,
Great Central Way, Rugby.
CV21 3XH
United Kingdom

www.ninearchespress.com

Printed in the United Kingdom by:
Imprint Digital

Nine Arches Press is supported using public funding by Arts Council England.

Supported using public funding by
ARTS COUNCIL
ENGLAND

Contents

Sevenling

I dress like my idea of a boy:
creased trousers & pea coats & good shoes,
things the world expects of me.

I'd love to paint my eyes & nails
& skin the colour of dusk & blood & sky
be beautiful for a moment, dropping

expectations like a coat on a dance floor.

A Boy Becomes a Brooding Hen

A boy wants a baby, dreams of being a father, stuffs
footballs up his jumper & practises midlife crises,
crocodile tears in the shower. He wants to lay an egg
but looks down at his body, presses his belly outward:
moon held in his hands, listens to the water under his
skin. He imagines himself running with a buggy,
looks at his friends with babies, is jealous of their
casual fatherhood, their Sundays & car keys. He
thinks he'd like to have a boy and for that boy to be
a dancer. He touches his nipples and asks *what are
these? Memories of the parent I could have been when I
was a half-formed thing, sexless & drifting in water.*

The Partridges

          take off with the same anxious
engine-flap of wings you hear
from topless boys on mopeds

who fly together up
a high road in August, t-shirts
fluttering round shoulders.

In autumn the partridges
do not know they are being
hunted or that this hum-thrum-beat

of their wing-machines is good
as a car horn for the mouths
of the shotguns. The partridges

are too slow & stupid to survive
so they feather-drum
into the shout of the guns

swallowed whole by the scatter-pattern
leaving the silence of a crashed
moped behind them.

A Boy Becomes a Mandrake

A boy is born screaming, his knotted root face
wrenched from the good, clean earth. Before he was
skin he was green, before he was bone he was bark.
Shouting from his bed, gasping for water before milk.
Scream & writhe is the only language he is capable of
so far. It was lonely in the soil but to be pulled from the
packed dirt's dark hug with no warning is even worse.
Now the only thing he knows each day is there will be
morning & hunger again & again.

Small Hands

We hug on the only chair left in the classroom,
       high-pitched love & no fight.
We are so small that our bottoms
       fit on the same dip of red plastic.

We are only vaguely aware of the distance
       men are supposed to keep,
how silence should stretch between us
       like an Achilles meeting muscle & bone.

If we could, we would hug & kiss
       as girls do, hold hands on the way to lessons,
comment on the ebb of our bodies,
       note how pretty our hands can be,

the curve of each other's hips,
       the fit of shirts on our skinny ribs.
It would be perfect because
       it hasn't happened like this before.

A Boy Runs

out of his lungs like they are a coat held by a parent at a school gate. The world around him is closing, the shops pulling down shutters as he turns into a cemetery where his heels push the dead further into their graves. He feels his weight on the ankle that crumpled beneath him months ago. He didn't listen to the physio or do the exercises she gave him. He hoped he would heal himself, *that in deepening the wound he would make it more heroic*, grow back into the bruised ligaments till his breathing was a spooked horse again, spittle rattling from his cheeks, the bit between his teeth worn away by worrying. The whip of hundreds of fathers keeping him going, *going, going*.

Tense

Hugging my brother
is like holding a tennis racket
to your chest

his ribs
taut strings
his shoulder blades arching

like a racket's frame
the tendons in his neck
stretching the skin.

Thin as he is I find it
difficult to fit
language around him.

I worry about
the world pressing
down on his body.

When I hug him
I am careful
of his ribs

the breath beneath.
I remind myself
this is not a game.

Boys Play Football

and they argue over who will be goalkeeper.
The older boy wins by kicking his brother in the groin.
The younger boy crumples, burst football of a brother
in the winter sunshine. This small crime is allowed
between boys who would once be bathed together.
The body will be hidden, the untidy shed of childhood
holding the cadaver. When their father comes looking
after hearing a whimpering, the older boy refuses to
answer, says only that he is not his brother's keeper.

Field Dressing a Rabbit

The defensive linesman does
another 10 reps. He's put on 20lbs
since last season, now a rabbit
trussed up in uniform before being
cut from sternum to perineum. The dark smell
of his offal floats across the field
and his body steams as his back thumps
against grass and he does another 20 crunches.
The coach pulls out his guts turning
his belly into muscle, skinning him
in the heat, un-seaming the tendon
from bone, cutting at his hind quarters
– the dark pink back straps, the best parts –
ignoring how tender he could be.

A Boy Sees a Ghost

and it is his father, his grandfather, his uncle, his brother, his friends, his bullies, his maths teacher, his reflection, all making faces through the window. They seem to be getting closer & closer, the boys he knew from school who used to get their dicks out in English, died, went to heaven, now wanking ectoplasm all over some seraphim. They walk through walls and over battlements, rain clouds & hecklers in the audience. They are slipknots & bloody Banquos, innocent & full of sin, unbaptised babies in limbo, shimmering. Some killed themselves, others died of embarrassment. *Oh Boy Oh Boy Oh Boy,* what a time to be a boy under forty-five, what a time to not be alive.

Parliament Hill Lido

The clockwork of my father's body wakes him at 6am,
pulls him by the eyelids out of bed toward the swim,

even in December dawn-drunk lunatics gather on goose-pimpled tiles,
the moon still floating, a lonely body in the sky.

The slap of water rearranges his synapses and as his feet kick
the ripple, his veins turn a serrated blue.

When I tell people about my father and his weirdness
I don't mention how he speaks less if not for swimming

or those mornings when he returns
hair still wet, the blood bright in his cheeks,

how we cross on the doorstep both trying
to stay in our lane, our bodies in sharper focus.

A Boy Turns Ten

and he has the mind of a twenty-year-old but the temper of a two-year-old. He breaks things & shouts, almost bursts blood vessels, keeps getting in fights at school, teachers have to restrain him. He gets Jack in a headlock and they slow dance outside the Year 5 classroom with no sense of the consequences. He picks up a bad habit, begins to write swear words on walls in the boys' toilet; *fuck*, he writes, *shit*, and the feeling of transgression is weighty, the felt-tipped badness, how he disguises his handwriting so no one can trace it back to him. He takes this swooping feeling and learns to replace the violence in his hands with writing.

Scrum

Men packed tight:
       half hug, half fight,

Each knuckle
       gripping a numbered shirt

is another wrinkle
       as the ball trembles

in the sack of arched backs.
               They must check

themselves, a bump
       or push can break

a spine, form
       a lump.

A Boy Gets a Hand Job

Park-perfect dark midnight and swing keeping time, a girl with GCSEs & serious kissing technique, her blue shirt turned black by the night & the rain, holds a boy by the waist. The park is the only place they can go and feel safe enough to be unsafe, where the rain learns their shapes and they hear the hum of the café's corrugated iron roof. She slips him out of his denim-day and kisses him, opens the night sky of her hands and holds him like a cloud, no-one around to judge or verify for him that this is really happening. Something metallic sings – speakers in the distance pulsing – interrupting how unbecoming he is being. He is not sure what to do with his hands as she pulls him into the night, toward the one lit lamppost in the park.

The Cuckoos

after Liz Berry

In the penalty box
the boys are a nest of cuckoos
pushing each other out.
They feather as they leap

for the ball, arms beating
against the wind,
studded boots callousing
into claws. The ball spins

away, a white egg
flecked with blue
and they swoop after it,
wings opening in their chests.

Their hearts flutter past
the goalposts tattered
with Scotch tape, and over
a fence that has collapsed
like a weak back four.

Fuckboy

Found poem

He gets called a *fuckboy,* texts a friend asking for a
definition: **A fuckboy she says just wants to fuck, but
he's a millennial so is angsty about it. Has mummy
issues & a Soundcloud page. Roughly translated a
fuckboy is distressed denim & a pint of IPA. See
also: hipster; ex-boyfriend; Freelance Creative.
Often called Dylan, or Ben, or Killian. A fuckboy
explains what feminism means then blames you
for his erectile dysfunction. He fails to make plans
until he's certain you are D.T.F. He sleeps with you
and creeps out like they do in the movies. He looks
like he should be more solid than he is. He explains
the wine list and insists that – whilst *Mean Girls*
is a great film – *Goodfellas* has more artistic merit.
He brings you back to his bedroom and makes you
think *'why does every boy want to fuck me on those
navy blue sheets?'* A fuckboy is a lost bunch of keys,
no emotional labour and gaslights till it hurts.** He
copies and pastes the text into a word document,
takes credit for the hard work.

The Weasel

slips in front of me
slick as piss on the path.

I don't see its details but I hear
its teeth, its muscles stiff with power,

I feel the shiver of its eye
and the flick of its blood-heavy body.

How can something so small
be carnivorous? How

is this mustelid different
from the tame ferret you see

on a lead in the centre of town
or the smooth otter that charms

the rivers of the internet with its paws?
I flinch at the stain the weasel leaves

as it escapes from grass that parts
like a zip, a mouse clamped in its jaws.

A Boy is a Poet

with clean skin & combed hair & no neuroses, only the work, managing to apply himself to it fully, understanding the fluidity, managing a balance between art & financial viability. This boy's desk is a mess. When interviewed he says *yeah, no, mess is actually a part of my process.* His mother & father die the minute he puts them in a poem. He kills his darlings and his best friend along with them. Would he be happier as a policeman or a glassblower or a mechanic? His hands couldn't hack it. Do they all lie as much as he does? He is an actor, a bad one. He is never finished, simply abandoned. He shaves his head, wears baggy shirts & ripped jeans & quotes Bukowski un-ironically & worries & feels ashamed & lies about not having neuroses, and when someone asks what sort of writing he does he flusters, says *it's journalism mostly.*

Horses

My father becomes a mare
his hands a horse's nose pushing

under my winded stomach
helping me to my feet.

He raises my hands
above my head like a foal

looking up at the sky
for the first time. Unsteady

my father walks beside me
his hand nudging my side.

A Boy in a Blue Suit

In the changing room, a boy strips down to his boxers before folding himself into a new three-piece skin. Mirrors bounce this boy back at himself. He pulls his trousers up, buckles. He looks at his blue, blue, blue shape and mimes all possible movement: reaches, bends, dances. He whispers a secret to himself, *boy, you look beautiful,* as he buttons himself into the ocean and brushes his waves of flesh. He braces for the outside world, prepares for the *ooooooooos* & *aaaaaaahhs* like he is the spark of blue in the middle of every flame.

Mackerel Fishing

The sky's hair is flecked with grey
and fishermen are showing us

how to hook a life
spear it through the mouth

lift it breathless onto the deck.
My brother is first to catch a mackerel.

Cold & twitching, we celebrate
the last minutes of its life

whilst Dad sits apart, his hands
gripping the bench, knuckles white,

shaking like an engine,
taking long, deep breaths.

He'd wanted to catch a fish,
to run his hands through water,

scoop the grey-blue in his palm
but now he won't talk to anyone.

We pretend we haven't noticed
and turn our eyes back to the sea.

Boy Wonder

responds to panic lights in the night sky, beating criminals to a pulp in his mind. *BIFF! BANG! BOFF! POW!* Boy Wonder wakes each morning covered in a cloud of bruises he is forced to hide. He tries to redress himself, goes to Topman in search of something scarlet or forest green, loses the sculpted plastic, the fire proof cape. *Holy Fragility Batman!* he shouts, revelling in his capacity to be afraid, telling himself that *to be Robin is to give honour where there has always been shame.*

Shadow Boxing

the boy fighting ghosts // in his back garden will never
know // that his punches // have landed in my poem
// in the skin & bone of winter // dressed in a string
vest & cotton bottom shorts // he works the body of
nothingness // his gloves glancing off the cheekbone
of air // breaking December's icy jaw // he rests hands
on thighs // trying to catch the breath // that keeps
disappearing from his lungs // does he think // about
what he is punching // or is the swing enough // the
air resistance // I write every jab & twitch // reach out
towards him // trying to catch something before it hits
// the ground // a boy who doesn't know // what he is
hitting // let alone why

Frightened Rabbit

Gone boy, boy lost but still running, trainers pounding the ground, looking for a river: frightened rabbit, Richey Edwards & Jeff Buckley. *No, this can't be the way it ends.*

Chandler from Friends, Ross not knowing how to be lonely because we can't all fuck like Joey. We so rarely know our bodies; we might drown in our own bloodstream. Wiped clean surfaces.

Blood, sunlight, darkness sits with you in the pub. Grab life by the free porn. Wine & whiskey & clean white shirts that don't show the hurt.

Our bodies are piano keys that girls press softly. They are rubbing the skin from our knuckles whilst we beg for attention. **One study reveals a rise in men with erectile dysfunction.**

Fist-language, knuckles leave speech marks: torn shirts, *Die Hard*, wife-beater vests. We know our best dressed heroes by what they have done to their partners.

Frightened rabbits, fights in the street. *Why me?* Cry, football, cry, rugby. *This is the first time you've hugged me.* Granddad in the navy, boy in the club, we all have tequila salt in our wounds, baby.

Punch drunk, hunched up, dumb luck, club shuts. The battery on our phones runs red as blood, shout when you think you've had enough, we will keep going anyway. We need to talk gut,

but what we
talk is bullshit, dog bark, frightened rabbit. Language is beyond
our grasp and we would be talking too loud in all this music. Men
all put their hands to the earth and say sorry *but*.

We know that our
muscles look best in shadow, sweet as bruised apples. Stressed
millennial, moisturiser & shaving cream, cut-throat razors trying
to save us from ourselves.

Pink button-down, garish tie. Every colour
does some violence to the eye; every father does some violence to
the boy; every boy does some violence to themselves. *Dying is safer
than saying what I feel.*

Get your prostate checked, shrug on coats
of muscle, bulletproof denim, bad dreams & broken ankles,
depression battles fought with toy swords & water pistols.

Pray
to God, look up to heaven, brave new haircut: David Beckham.
Barber shaved too close to the skin, you can see our raw pinkness,
our baby faces. We cut ourselves on blades of grass,

the world, a knife held to our throats.

The Pennine Way

Thin as the air this high up, my father runs ahead
leaving me in his wake.

Over crags, past sheep who moan
almost human into the air heavy with rain

the wind sprints
through gaps in the stone walls

and I try to pull breath through the cold
tunnel of my nostrils.

Look at him at the top of the hill,
carrying nothing but house keys & breath.

Nom De Guerre

*'Someone starts a game which gives us
a porn star's nom de guerre. It calls
for mothers' maiden names, involves first
pets...'*
  – Tiffany Atkinson

Not even my mother would recognise me
from this angle: how I see myself, straight down
looking over the sun of my stomach.

I'm no Jon Dough, Peter North or Tommy Gunn
but I still see through a screen, me in another life,
the knot & stitch of my body pulled tight to the camera

making sure I'm well developed. In this life
I go like clockwork, hard rock & tick tock
stopped only by the yell of *cut* –

how much of my body is left
in the editing suite? The camera follows me
from the set, catches me on my off days

when I'm not ready to fuck: sweating
unscripted & flaccid. How will I be christened
with only a cock and three blunt syllables to my name?

Boy in Various Poses

The boy is an orange, an apple, a banana, a portrait
by one of the Dutch masters, his armpit, a water lily,
his dick, the sunflowers. He tries not to move so his
twitch won't break someone's line. His back is arched
so he won't look so fat, so the light won't catch his
acne scars. They asked him to keep his shoes on, black
leather boots beneath a body scuffed by living. He
can't see the sketches but feels the paint slipping down
the stretch-marked canvas like beads of sweat from his
temple. He feels himself up on the easel, cross-legged
& naked, his spit turned to acrylic, his peach soft skin,
arsehole pink & dark as the pip.

Advice from the Quarterback

It can be easy to hide. Five concussions
in fourteen months. *Just keep your mouth shut*
and your head down, test the limit of your bone.
Stay away from people who'd think you have one, keep quiet,

just try to go out there and function as all men do,
day after day, our ears ringing from colliding
so hard with the world. Sometimes I get
so angry, so blind. *Everybody knows*

it is a dangerous game, padded rage hurtling at you,
the fear before connection. But *the game has done*
so much for me, filled my blood with grit & cortisone,
it's made me who I am. My father said he worries

that I am *so tough, such a competitor,* that I might say
I'm OK when I'm not OK. I mustn't worry
after throwing five hundred yards & four touchdowns
in a 40-37 victory *that I barely remember the game.*

A Boy with Haemorrhoids

How much blood was there? the doctor asks the boy, *more or less than a teaspoon?* He sees teabags splitting, spilling out. All this blood is awakening, so bright it sings off the sheet music of ripped skin, his sphincter a microphone unable to hold the plosive popping, a blood clot turning a purple shade of thrombosis. His veins are a balloon on the edge of bursting. He realises that seam of unlaced tissue was a peep hole into ageing, the first time a doctor pressed a finger against his most sensitive opening. *How much blood?* The doctor asks again and he wants to tell her it was like open heart surgery of the arse, wants to ask how something so small holds so much colour in.

Butchery

On the wall of the Beefeater
      someone's labelled a cow: its flank,
rib, chuck, sirloin, rump, shank.
      What uncertain meat hovers

between these sections? What tender
      gristle isn't served on a bank
of chips & peas? What goes unthanked?
      The eyelash that quivers

at the eye of the stun gun?
      The nostril twitching at the wound
of the abattoir, its dark rooms?
      The ear that hears the lonely thump

of its flank and feels the new dead-
      ness, twitch until it's beyond art?
Whatever goes unnamed, unloved,
      I want to know that part.

Flower Boy

A boy buys a bouquet but makes clear it's for his girlfriend. He feels the stigma carrying it home, the petal edges that close up in the cold. He wishes he was soaked in water feeling every inch of his flower body. His knuckles bloom in the morning air. He pricks himself on a thorn, the beauty pushing deep into his thumb. Blood makes a meniscus of red hovering at the end of his finger, small flower of its own. He sucks his thumb as he returns to his girlfriend, tastes its thick iron violence & slight perfume.

Wind

In bed our stomachs won't sit still.
Mine makes an uncontrolled dog squeak
when I'm stressed and your gut creaks
its slow machinery after too many lentils.

Tonight, I move your hand to the swell
of my belly so that your body heat
calms the tide of how unstoppably I eat,
cups the small food baby that I fell

pregnant with after one Sunday lunch.
I have never held someone close enough
before to smell the worst of them
but I want to press my ear to your abdomen

and hear through it, like it was a shell,
the sea of your body, what it has to tell.

A Boy Falls

out of bed, alone at night and suddenly remembers how much of a body he has. A body doesn't exist without a boy, just as no boy exists without a body. If no body is there for the boy, then is the boy even in his body? He worries he is missing the D, closes his eyes and feels the wood at the centre of him. The wrinkled bark of his foreskin, the opening like a knot in the trunk. He did not know he was beautiful here – he thought it was just another tree in the forest of his body, falling.

A&E

The doctor's been busy with heart attacks.
She's been washing the blood stuff
of Sunday night from her hands. This morning
a man is a sink plugged full of shame
and she has to find the best way
to hold his body, to bind his limbs
and adjust to the angle where he is most yawning
so she can pull out what is stuck
at the very base of him. Comfort
is no longer an option. He is lifted like a baby
having its nappy changed,
whilst his girlfriend waits
in the hall, wondering if he was elastic
enough when she slipped *it* in.
Was it the danger it posed that excited him?
Or did he feel like he was giving birth? Certainly
this was what made him feel alive. I love most
that it was a Monday when he found the pulse
of the morning, before work
when he wanted to bring some joy to his body.
He couldn't wait till the weekend to feel
the world move slightly inside him.

A Boy Does a Magic Trick

appears in a black suit & striped collared shirt,
a new tie & shows the crowd his empty palms. There
are doves in his pockets & aces up his sleeves. A rabbit
quivers inside the hat of his heart. Boys know sleight
of hand so people are always looking somewhere else
as their houses of cards fall apart: *pick a card, any card*
this boy says, vanishing into his own head, folding his
fingers together like iron rings, failing to escape the
box he has locked himself in, and being dumped into
the Thames. He is gasping but is so magic that no one
comes to help him.

Taxidermy

The girl at the party holds aloft her stuffed capuchin
and explains how you cut straight down the middle, suck
out the organs, like a foot coming out of a sock of skin,

then you stitch it back together. The brain, you dry up
with a chemical so it won't rot. Former Mr California
Rich Piana collapsed at 45 whilst having a haircut.

At the autopsy they found his heart & liver
were twice the weight of a regular man's. They sliced
into him, opened his sternum to see and I wonder

if they thought of stuffing him? Freezing his blue-white
eyes & bleached grin, putting his body on show
looking more real than he ever did in life.

A Boy Stands On Top of an Air Vent

A boy dyes his hair blonde bombshell; brown persists at the roots like blue veins under thin white skin but his cheeks are cherubic. He flutters his eyelashes in the mirror and thinks he is perfect, wearing that cologne someone bought him last Christmas. He has nothing on but the radio, feels free and pulls a white dress out of the cupboard where it has been hanging like a skeleton. He shaves off his beard, bringing the air closer to his skin. Standing on a street corner, the vent blowing on his balls, he is reminded of how much of a man he is.

Sleep Apnoea

for Eddie Hall

The world's strongest man
often stops breathing in his sleep.
He's so big he needs a machine
to lift his breath for him.

He can pull trains with his teeth,
deadlift trees, bicep-curl cars –
still he dreams of raising
aeroplanes above his head,
of bench-pressing the sky.

His eyeballs have popped
out of their sockets from the strain
like soap from wet hands.
His deltoids have been sucked
from pockets of bone.

Smaller men carry their children
like balloons, keep their wives awake
with the depth of their snores
but he tears phonebooks in half
when he doesn't know who to call.

His heart is a dumbbell
being lifted to a heavy beat
and at night he cannot feel himself
holding his breath too long.

Feather Boy

Someone found his body in the woods, edged in
fox spit & leaking squirrels, wrenched crisp packets
& aerosols, ring pulls & quiet killings, shotgun
cartridges & dog shit, beaters' sticks & laughing gas
canisters. His beak was cracked open and the earth
was in his mouth. Maybe it was a BB gun that got him,
or the mercy of a cat's clean teeth? It would be best
to leave his body alone but someone takes it home.
Makes a meal of plucking feather from bone, father
from son. Once stripped, his skeleton is sprayed
silver as a Christmas decoration, his ribcage, sternum
& skull laid out like tools on a work table. Someone
rearranges the body and leaves him hanging from the
ceiling unable to take flight.

Freddie The Lion

after Cai Draper

He stepped on my fucking tail. What was he trying
to convince me of? When you're a lion
and you've seen the things I've seen
you begin to wonder about transubstantiation
& metaphors. Feed me: his blood, my wine,
his skin, the Eucharist. Lions are all literalists.
Feed me that preacher wrapped in sunlight
like a pig in bacon at Christmas. Leave the stole
like skin on custard, this bastard doesn't pray
I can taste it. Feed me his godly eyeballs,
his holy groin, I will pick the salad
of his cassock out of my teeth.
Here he comes, dramatic Daniel for now
but soon a headless Baptist,
fallen in with my roar & muscle, my hot teeth
& circus tricks. He cracks a whip but I smell
the priest bricking it, been in the cage
less than a minute and is seriously lacking in courage.
And limbs. He fell to bits like a Bible when I ripped
out his spine. Forgive me father for I am a sinner,
it has been years since my last full dinner.
As he fell from his pulpit – his paradise – my cage
became the rude, unholy earth, my saliva, a flood.
I recognise eating him may not have been God's will
but I will rise again out of Norfolk soil,
out of drugged sleep, roll back the stone and explain
why the priest had to die. Years later look me up,
cat out of time. Google: Stiffkey. Priest. Lion.
You will see what I ate   and why.

Boys Audition to be Strippers

The bare lights on one boy's porky skin roast him pinker every minute he is under them. He watches the other boys being liquid on the stage and wishes he could dance, bicep & breathless, as women shout for the loss of his clothes, for the last strip, his thong a bacon rind torn off & chewed between their teeth. He looks in their eyes and sees his mother, those mornings when she used to dress him, the clothes still warm from the radiator. They watch as he undoes all her good work.

Tease

This dance is for you: 9pm, week nights,
when I spill out of tired jeans which lock
around my slippers. In the bedroom's spotlight
I pose: the incongruity of socks

and button-down shirt. I swing, a light
fitting in a grotty club, glistening as I rock
to the extractor fan's music. Tonight
I wiggle my hips, accidentally knock

my kneecap on the bed post which becomes
a pole for me to shiver against in the cold:
the bed sheets, a stage for these demonstrations,
your smile, a folded note slipped into my old

boxer shorts, hanging lax on thighs & bum
as I twist & turn & come undone.

Snowboy

Someone has put buttons on a boy's jacket, hunks of
coal, carrot nose, cold toes, a scarf wrapped around
his neck. He was not born but built out of sky &
ground, his body three balls of packed ice. He feels big
& lumpy round the middle, his eyes unlit coal – how
can his body be frozen but decorated with something
so flammable? A boy is cold inside but has been told
that's the way he should be, that to melt would be
inexcusably weak.

Red Shirt

after Robert Pinsky

The collar, the colour: red checks,
the seams coming undone,
your skin through open buttons,

the missing ones don't matter now
because this is just the shirt
you sleep in and I dream about.

The length fits you
like a dress, the thickness, warm
as another body on week nights.

The sleeves, the rolled cuffs.
I fall asleep in your bed, my arm turning
to a ghost beneath your body.

The hems, the loose stitches
fluttering like split ends, how you
move into my touch.

The moment when you take it off,
bare as a light bulb, your skin
a cold moon, and you are looking at me

like something wonderful or terrible
is happening and in this light
you won't tell me which.

Boys Do Push Ups

their bodies low to the earth like beetles, arms splayed pushing themselves up. One boy trembles but follows his routine, every day, the calendar setting out the weeks till summer, his hands knowing the psalm the body must say to be presentable. He imagines his biceps turning to pipe organs, the neat pews of his abdomen. The rugby coach in his brain shouts at him to go all the way to the ground and back up again. Even though he is ten years past that, he still knows exactly how to kneel, how to stretch his legs to plank behind him, to slowly lift, and then press down, his head nudging the floor as if praying.

Water Weight

Boxers regularly increase their risk
of head injury by losing
and gaining large amounts
of weight before bouts.

> *The current*
> *heavyweight champion of the world*
> *weighs in at 113 bags of sugar,*
> *just under a quarter*
> *of a thoroughbred horse,*
> *in the same range as a bathtub*
> *full of skin-blistering water.*

They drop those final pounds
through dehydration: wrapping
themselves in cling film, losing
water they have no intention of replacing.

> *This creates a sauna*
> *next to the skin, easing moisture*
> *from muscles, massaging*
> *wrinkles into fingerprints,*
> *and making the brain more susceptible*
> *to damage, the skull a smashed*
> *china plate.*

No one has ever considered
the brain to be a dry thing
but these men – thirsty as chalk – fear
weight more than dying.

A Boy Watches *Die Hard*

How does a boy become a man? Violence is hand-me-down torn clothes, *ho ho ho* now he has machine gun machismo. He pulls on a white vest and swings from scaffolding. He turns his fingers to guns loaded with bad decisions. The vault is full of sadness and he needs explosives to get it all out. He crawls through the vents of puberty and grows an oil slick beard, dirty adolescence & untidy thoughts. Violence is a VHS tape he watches again & again. Rewind to the shot of Alan Rickman as he falls like the first man into the arms of the flames. He doesn't know if he will be Hans Gruber or John MacClane.

Gifts

Watching a cat neatly ease a mouse apart
makes me think of you. How the blood glows
as her teeth sink in and she eats the heart
but leaves the gall bladder that she knows

is bitter, reminds me of that evening
at dinner when I told you about the night
I was so drunk that I was vomiting
and shitting myself at the same time.

I gave you that story the way the cat
leaves the gore of her hunt on the pillow
and it made you laugh so much that
you almost pissed yourself. This is love, to know

the contents of my stomach on the floor
if anything would make you want me more.

A Boy Becomes a Vegetarian

dumps the meat out of his diet, shits out the last remnants of steak. The grease seeps from his skin, the skinny redness leaving his bloodstream. His mother worries he will become too thin but he assures her that he replenishes the iron with spinach & kidney beans. He examines his abdomen, goes to the airing cupboard where boxers hang like plucked chickens & the curled calves of socks sit on the pipes. T-shirts hang loose as a carcass on a meat hook ready to cover the bones. He learns that no body is a static thing and that each morning he can fall in love with it all over again.

Shaving Tips

In *Lion*,   Dev Patel has patches in his beard,
       small coins of skin.   A woman holds Patel's face,
collecting these openings in her palms,   and
kisses him.   You can read the short
history of my kissing in the swirls & dips of my beard.
Shaving injures: blood & sunlight,   claws
& emergencies on skin. The boy at school with a full mane told me
about the razor's edge,   explained what it takes away.
My beard is four magpies,   the chin,
the moustache   & both of the cheeks. A patch of pale
skin is exposed under my jawline   like the bird's
white under-feathers.   Do you see how this beard,   autumn
& blonde,   rests on the shoulders of the women I love?
      My beard fights tooth & nail   as it ruptures
the cheek,   leaves it sore.
       Sometimes I am tempted
to get rid of it,   skin myself,   wear it as a pelt.
I oil my beard till it glistens,   till it is sandalwood & wet earth;
    bird & lion.   I spent years watching
        the new faces of boys like me,
       their roaring chins.

Boy, Undressing

The boy removes himself from his body, pulls off his shoulders, undoes his ribs, begins the slow unscrewing of hair from thighs, lining each strand up on the night stand and leaving him with a baby-baldness. He unlatches each ankle before removing his feet, the shins are delicate today as he shelves them carefully next to his kneecaps in the cupboard. Reaching into his gut he scoops out the day's ablutions and finds a clump of stress he did not know he was digesting. After brushing them, he puts his teeth on the sink next to the taps and places what's left of his spit into a small bowl. He drained his sweat, cum & blood earlier in the evening. His hair fits perfectly on the mannequin on his vanity table. Looking in the mirror he removes his beard, his chest, and – gently – his genitals. He falls into bed still wearing his thoughts.

Cues

for Tom

The pub's red and yellow glow holds us still,
our beer sitting cheap and quiet at our elbows.
Even the pool table's green stubble outgrows
our beards and in this light, we're beautiful.
Our bodies look for angles, negotiating shots,
I break the triangle's neat silence and we hear
the click of colours against one another.
We learn when to be powerful, when to be soft.
I want to win but not for this to end, not now,
when I'm passing the last cue left on the shelf
to a boy I'm so close with I could be playing myself.
The knock of white on red, the hum of yellow
rolling to the edge, the scrape of cue and blue chalk.
I want to notice the space that's left and fill it with our talk.

A Boy Gets Married

and the wedding is beautiful, the cake incredible. He glows at the centre of it all in a red dress & sexy garter. At his side is his father, giving him away, his mother crying in the pew. The priest doesn't know what to do with this boyish face at the altar so just gets on with it. It is a fairy tale, a pumpkin for a carriage, but he knew this would be a different kind of marriage: less silk & lace more heather & thistle, no white dress, more arterial. Find him in the forest: something cold, something true, something foraged, something new.

Notes

A Boy Runs: Reworks a lines from Terrance Hayes, 'the deeper the wound the more heroic the healing' *(American Sonnets for My Past and Future Assassin,* Penguin, 2019*).*

Fuckboy: The majority of the text of 'Fuckboy' was contributed to this book by Dr Samantha Purvis.

Boy Wonder: The final line is a reworking of a quote from Maggie Nelson's *The Argonauts*, 'to be femme is to give honour where there has always been shame' (*The Argonauts*, Canongate, 2015).

Frightened Rabbit: Includes a quotation from Goethe, 'every colour does some violence to the eye.' (Johann Wolfgang Goethe, *Theory of Colours*, MIT Press, 1970).

Nom De Guerre: The quotation from Tiffany Atkinson comes from her book *Kink and Particle,* Seren, 2006.

Advice from the Quarter Back: The italics are extracts from Clint Tricket's interview in the New York Times in November 2015 and reported speech from his appearance in the documentary series *Last Chance U.*

Acknowledgements

With thanks to the following publications where several of these poems or younger versions of them appeared: *84: Poems on Male Suicide, The Result is What You See Here Today, Elbow Room, The Darker Side of Love Anthology, Great Britain Anthology, Ambit, Magma, The Rialto, Ink, Sweat and Tears, Lighthouse Journal, Bath Magg, perverse, Mechanics Institute Review* and *Oxford Poetry*.

'Field Dressing a Rabbit' won the Winchester Poetry Prize 2020, 'A Boy Sees a Ghost' came third in the Winchester Poetry Prize 2019 and 'Sevenling' came third in the *Magma* Poetry Competition 2017.

Thanks to Jane and Angela at Nine Arches Press for their support, creativity and belief. Thanks to First Story, The Poetry Society, Spread the Word, The National Centre for Writing and Poetry School who have all helped me emotionally, administratively and financially over the years. In particular, thanks to Hannah Garrard, Victoria Maitland, Chris Gribble, Sam Ruddock, Peggy Hughes, Daisy Dockrill, Jay Bhadricha, Milly Hirst, Rowan Whiteside, Lucy Farrant, and Pasco-Q Kevlin. Thank you to Mónica Parle and her family – James, Rafa and Isa. Thank you to Michael Bolger for always loving my work. Thank you to Laura Kenwright for the texts, the phone calls, the love and for being on email.

Thanks to Nathalie Teitler, Ella Frears, Erin Bolens, Denise Riley, Meryl Pugh, Kim Moore, Alan Buckley, Hannah Jane Walker, Rishi Dastidar, Ross Raisin, Helen Mort, Polarbear, Hannah Lowe and Ali Lewis who have all read poems, given me feedback, been on trains home from gigs with me and supported me for years.

Thank you to my Mum and my Dad for filling my life with books. Thank you to my siblings Imogen and Lester for being at the end of a phone. Thank you to my army of aunts and my grandma for always being in the front row. Thank you to my friends Sam Purvis, Cadi Cliff and Tom Bingham. Thank you to Harriet Creelman, I'm glad I cried at your wedding. Finally, thank you to Daisy, for everything.